JOSHUA MOVES TO THE JUNGLE

JOSHUA MOVES TO THE JUNGLE

DAWN BAIRD

ILLUSTRATED BY KRISTEN POLSON

REDEMPTION PRESS

© 2017 by Dawn Baird. All rights reserved.

Published by Redemption Press, PO Box 427, Enumclaw, WA 98022

Toll Free (844) 2REDEEM (273-3336)

Redemption Press is honored to present this title in partnership with the author. The views expressed or implied in this work are those of the author. Redemption Press provides our imprint seal representing design excellence, creative content, and high quality production.

No part of this publication may be reproduced, stored in a retrieval system, or transmitted in any way by any means—electronic, mechanical, photocopy, recording, or otherwise—without the prior permission of the copyright holder, except as provided by USA copyright law.

The Scripture quotation is taken from THE HOLY BIBLE, ENGLISH STANDARD VERSION®, copyright© 2001 by Crossway, a publishing ministry of Good News Publishers. Used by permission.

Illustrated by Kristen Polson

ISBN 13: 978-1-68314-499-1 (Paperback)
         978-1-68314-500-4 (Hard Cover)

Library of Congress Catalog Card Number: 2017955631

Dedication

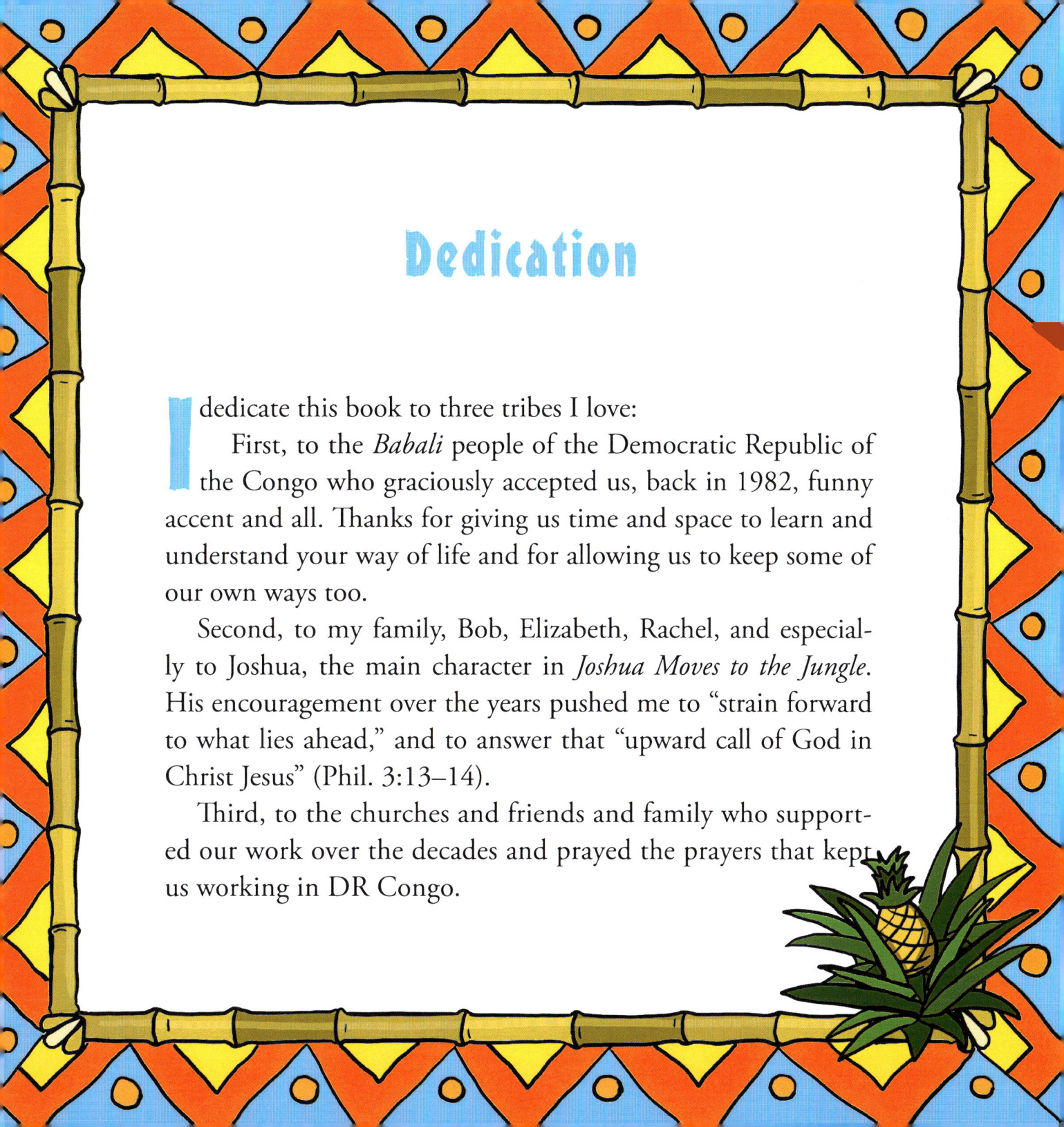

I dedicate this book to three tribes I love:

First, to the *Babali* people of the Democratic Republic of the Congo who graciously accepted us, back in 1982, funny accent and all. Thanks for giving us time and space to learn and understand your way of life and for allowing us to keep some of our own ways too.

Second, to my family, Bob, Elizabeth, Rachel, and especially to Joshua, the main character in *Joshua Moves to the Jungle*. His encouragement over the years pushed me to "strain forward to what lies ahead," and to answer that "upward call of God in Christ Jesus" (Phil. 3:13–14).

Third, to the churches and friends and family who supported our work over the decades and prayed the prayers that kept us working in DR Congo.

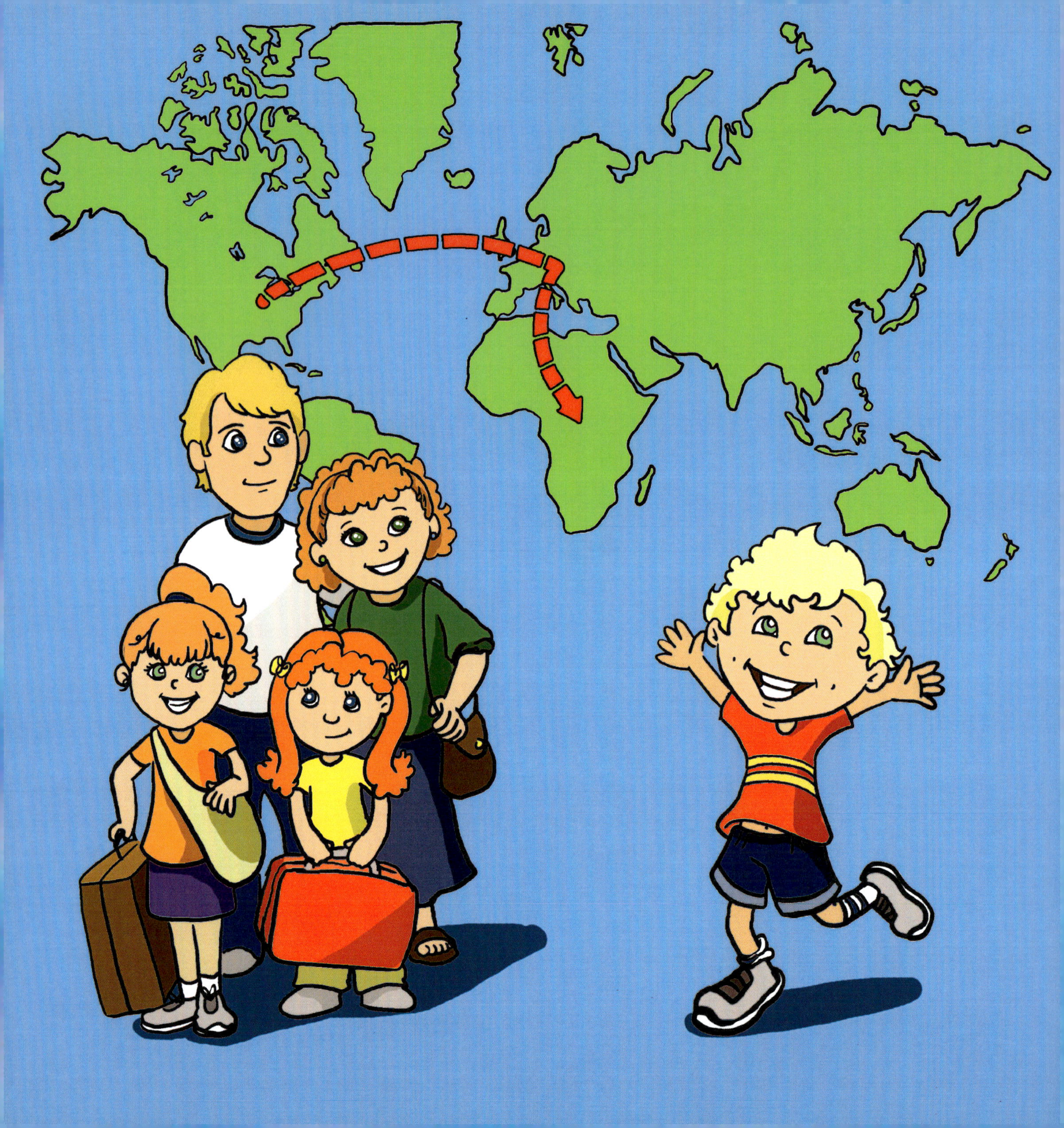

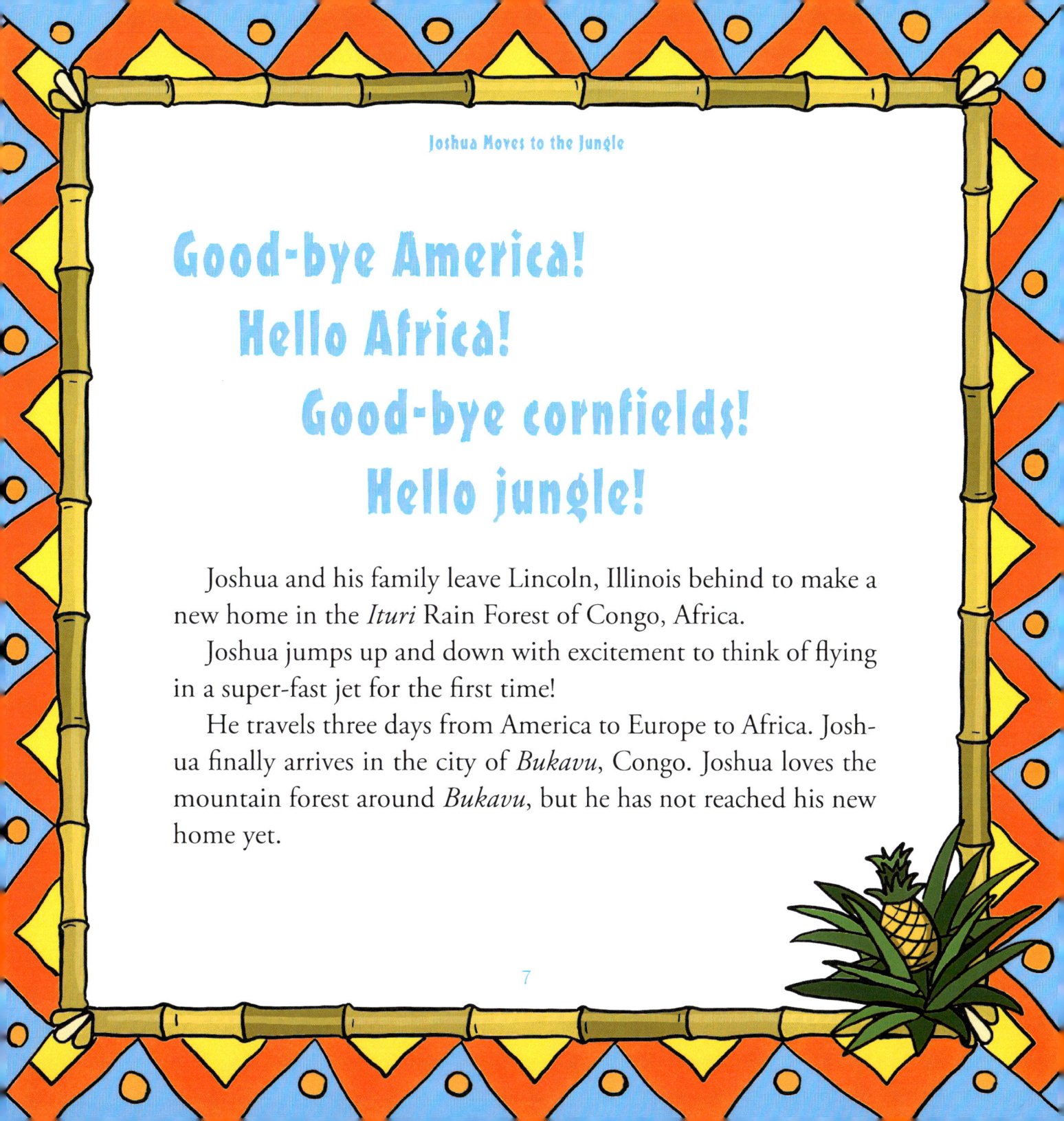

Joshua Moves to the Jungle

Good-bye America!
Hello Africa!
Good-bye cornfields!
Hello jungle!

Joshua and his family leave Lincoln, Illinois behind to make a new home in the *Ituri* Rain Forest of Congo, Africa.

Joshua jumps up and down with excitement to think of flying in a super-fast jet for the first time!

He travels three days from America to Europe to Africa. Joshua finally arrives in the city of *Bukavu*, Congo. Joshua loves the mountain forest around *Bukavu*, but he has not reached his new home yet.

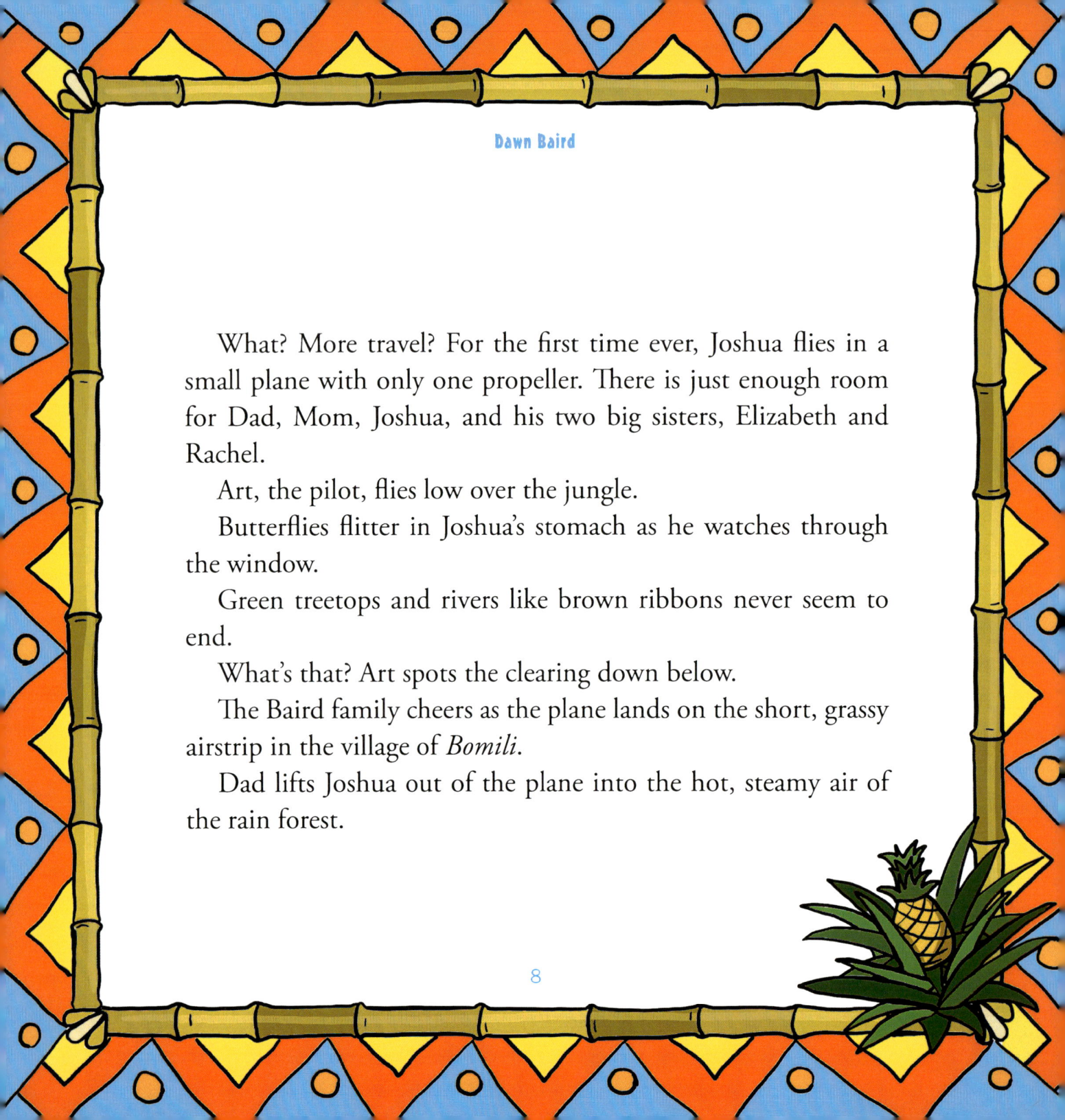

Dawn Baird

What? More travel? For the first time ever, Joshua flies in a small plane with only one propeller. There is just enough room for Dad, Mom, Joshua, and his two big sisters, Elizabeth and Rachel.

Art, the pilot, flies low over the jungle.

Butterflies flitter in Joshua's stomach as he watches through the window.

Green treetops and rivers like brown ribbons never seem to end.

What's that? Art spots the clearing down below.

The Baird family cheers as the plane lands on the short, grassy airstrip in the village of *Bomili*.

Dad lifts Joshua out of the plane into the hot, steamy air of the rain forest.

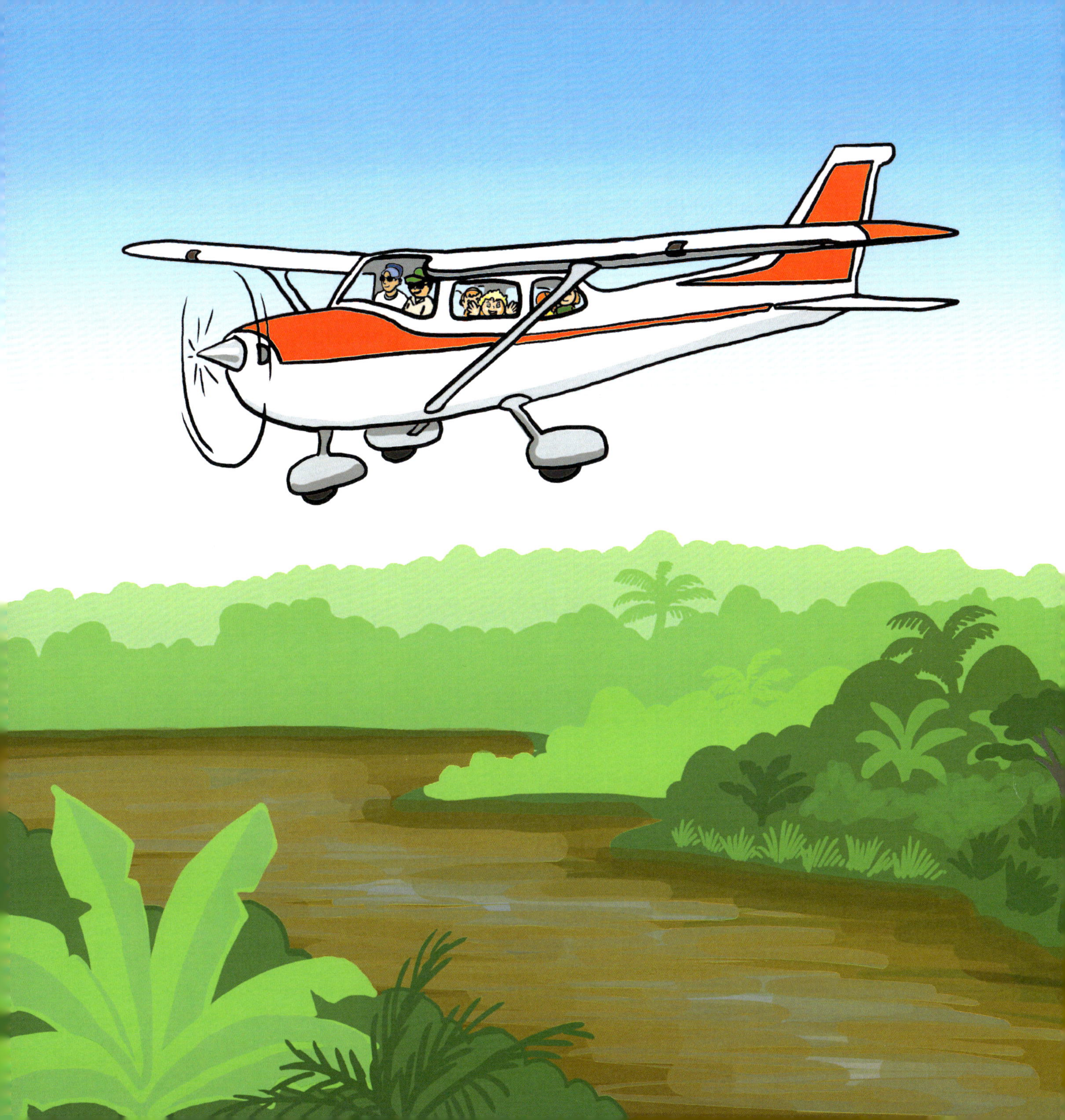

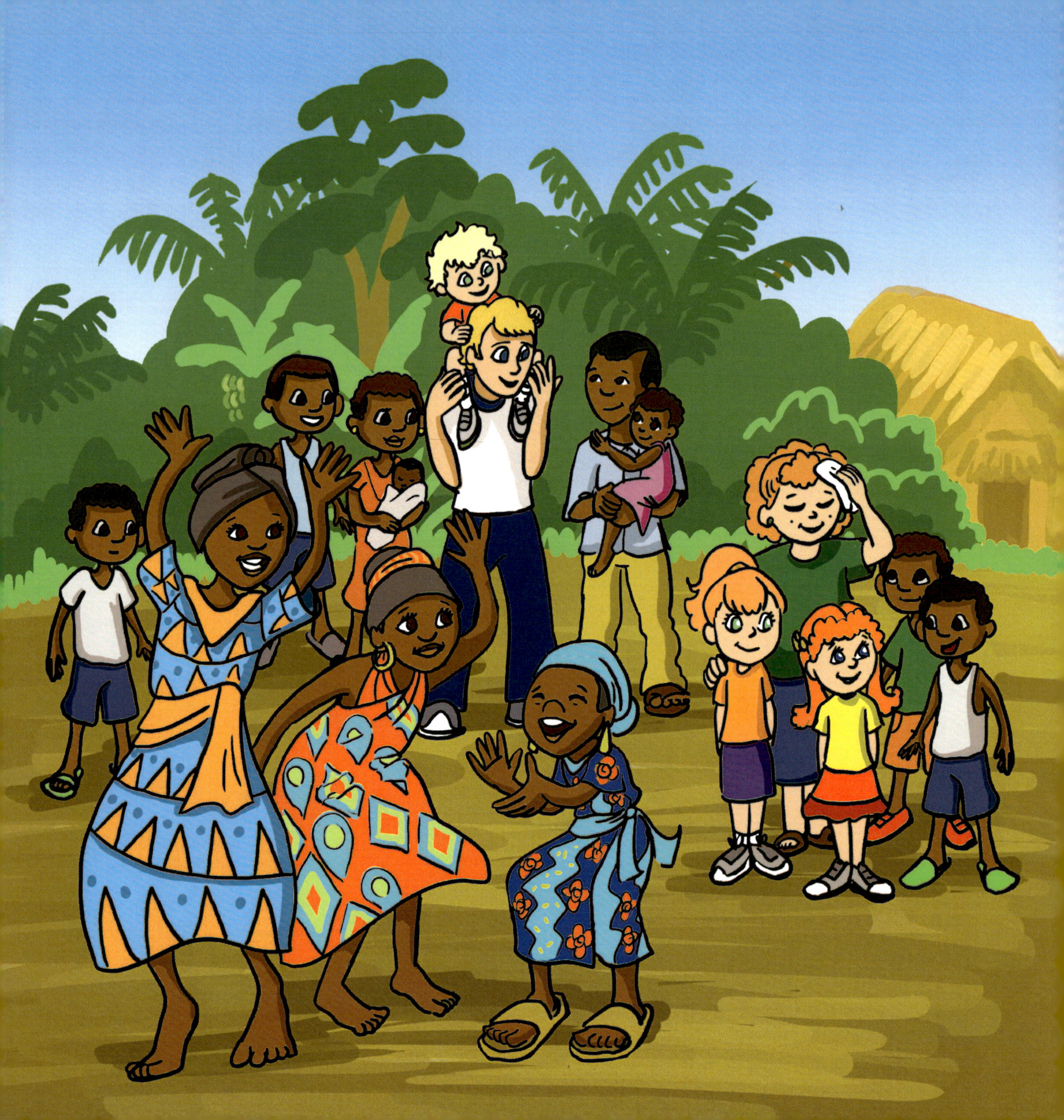

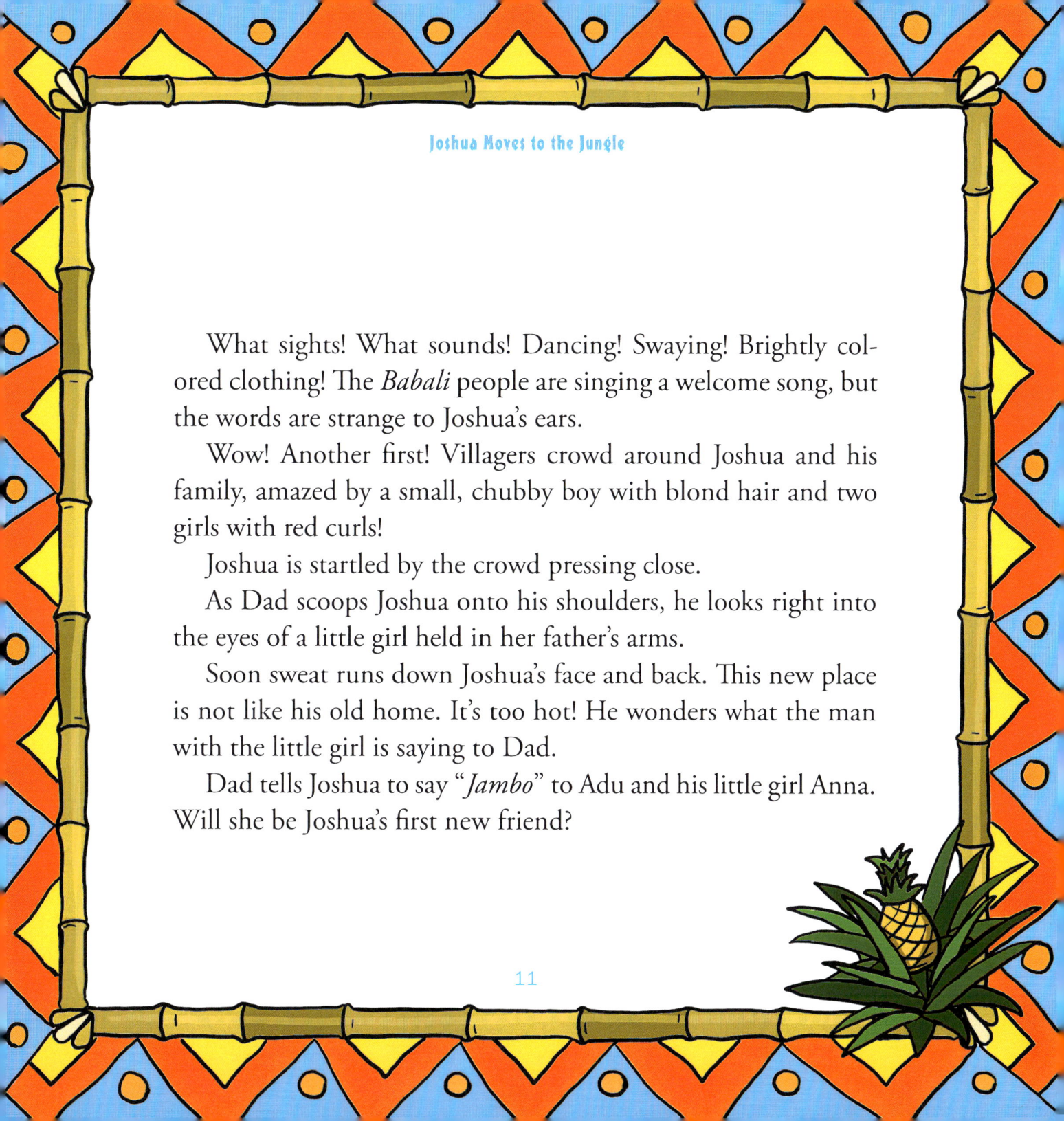

Joshua Moves to the Jungle

What sights! What sounds! Dancing! Swaying! Brightly colored clothing! The *Babali* people are singing a welcome song, but the words are strange to Joshua's ears.

Wow! Another first! Villagers crowd around Joshua and his family, amazed by a small, chubby boy with blond hair and two girls with red curls!

Joshua is startled by the crowd pressing close.

As Dad scoops Joshua onto his shoulders, he looks right into the eyes of a little girl held in her father's arms.

Soon sweat runs down Joshua's face and back. This new place is not like his old home. It's too hot! He wonders what the man with the little girl is saying to Dad.

Dad tells Joshua to say "*Jambo*" to Adu and his little girl Anna. Will she be Joshua's first new friend?

Adu points to a mud building just beyond the airstrip. The Baird family learns this is their new home. At the front door, a dim coolness welcomes Joshua. The sweat on his face begins to dry.

Wow! Another first for Joshua! His new house is made of mud plastered onto woven vines and capped with clusters of long brown leaves. The leaves hang halfway down the screened windows to keep out rain and the hot glare of the midday sun.

But where is the bathroom? The Baird family chuckles at the sight of their outdoor toilet called a *choo*.

This is going to be a new and different way to live.

Mom and Dad are happy in this house, so Joshua is happy too.

But Joshua learns of a danger. No more going barefoot. He must beware of thorns and spiders that bite. Joshua must get used to always wearing shoes or flip-flops.

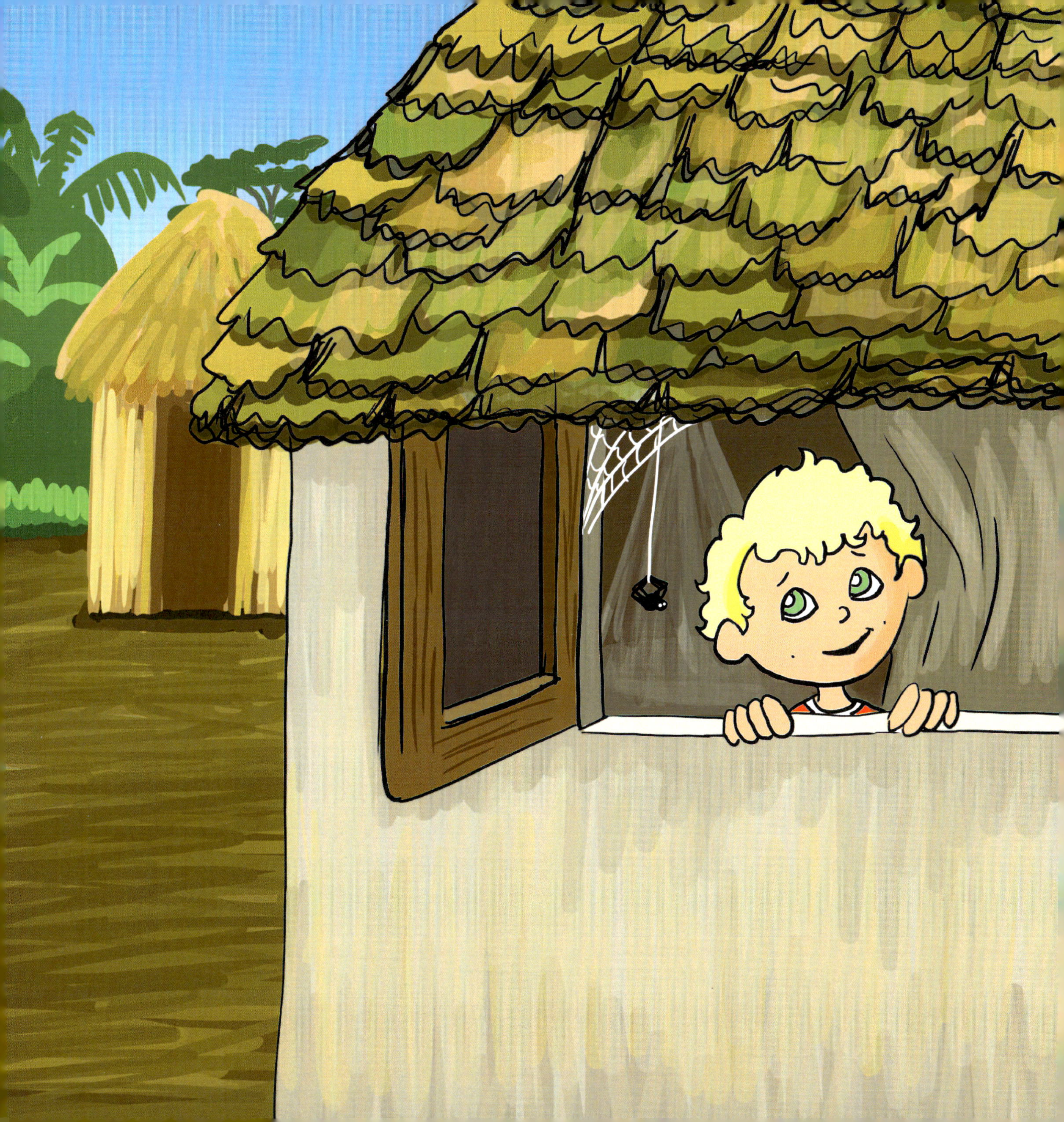

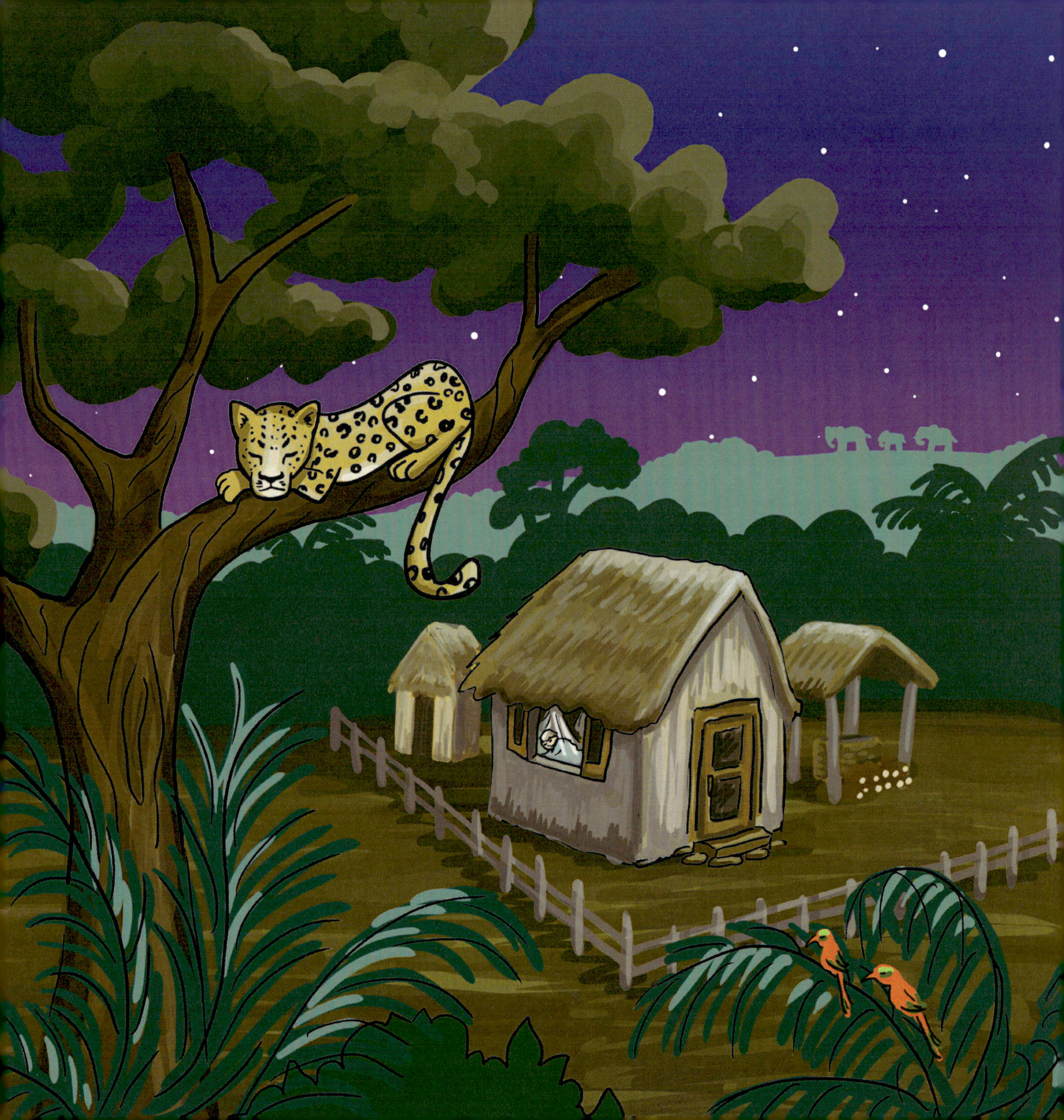

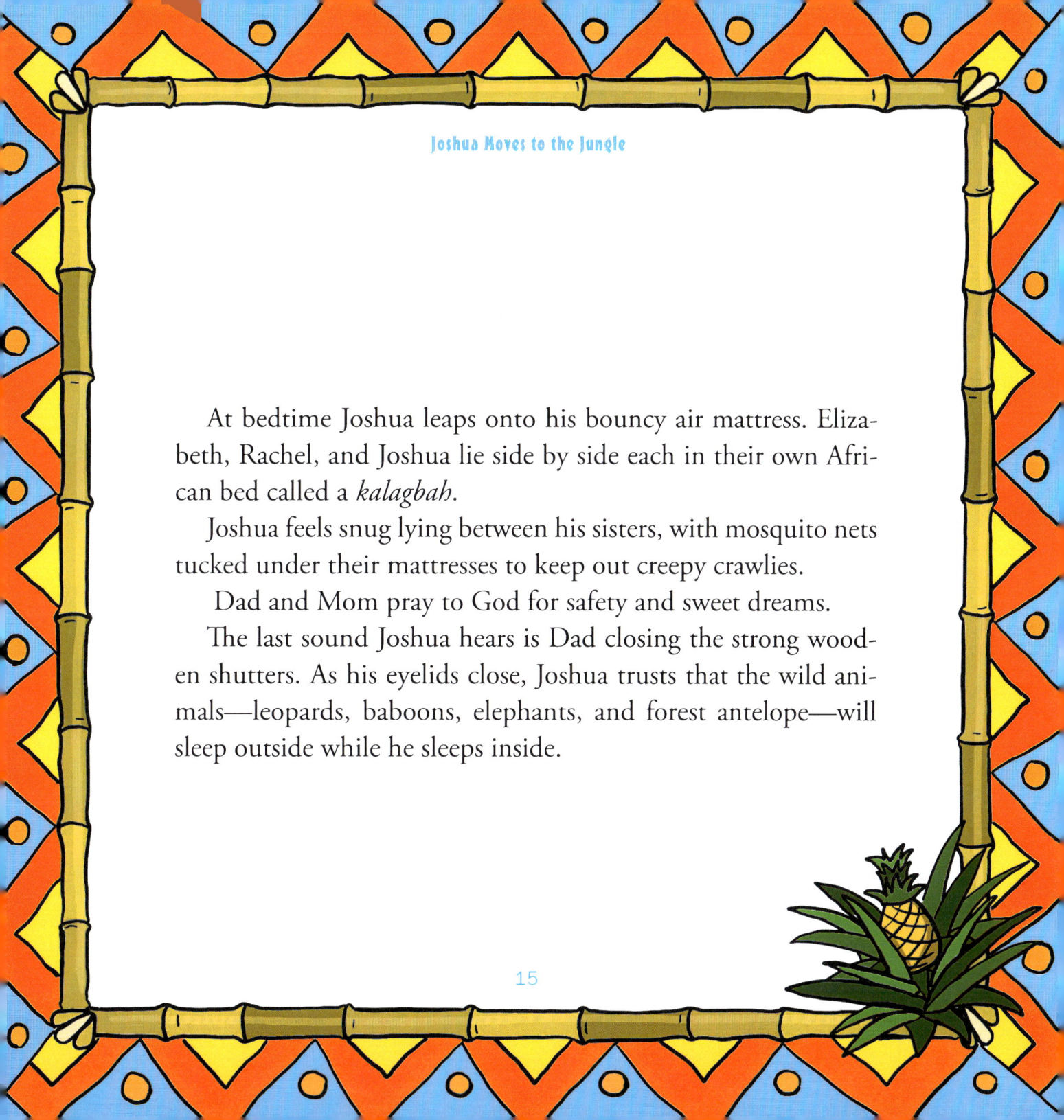

Joshua Moves to the Jungle

At bedtime Joshua leaps onto his bouncy air mattress. Elizabeth, Rachel, and Joshua lie side by side each in their own African bed called a *kalagbah*.

Joshua feels snug lying between his sisters, with mosquito nets tucked under their mattresses to keep out creepy crawlies.

Dad and Mom pray to God for safety and sweet dreams.

The last sound Joshua hears is Dad closing the strong wooden shutters. As his eyelids close, Joshua trusts that the wild animals—leopards, baboons, elephants, and forest antelope—will sleep outside while he sleeps inside.

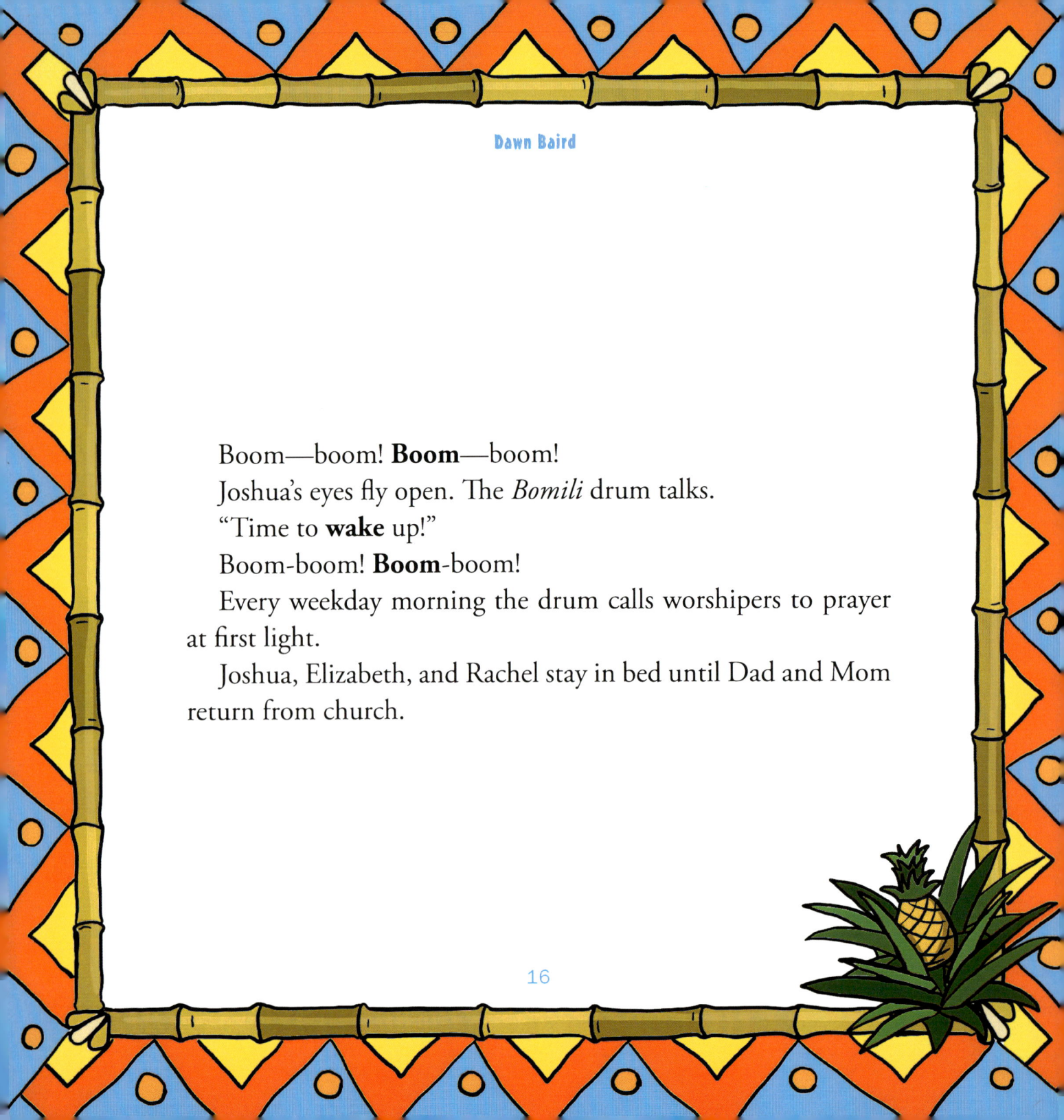

Dawn Baird

Boom—boom! **Boom**—boom!

Joshua's eyes fly open. The *Bomili* drum talks.

"Time to **wake** up!"

Boom-boom! **Boom**-boom!

Every weekday morning the drum calls worshipers to prayer at first light.

Joshua, Elizabeth, and Rachel stay in bed until Dad and Mom return from church.

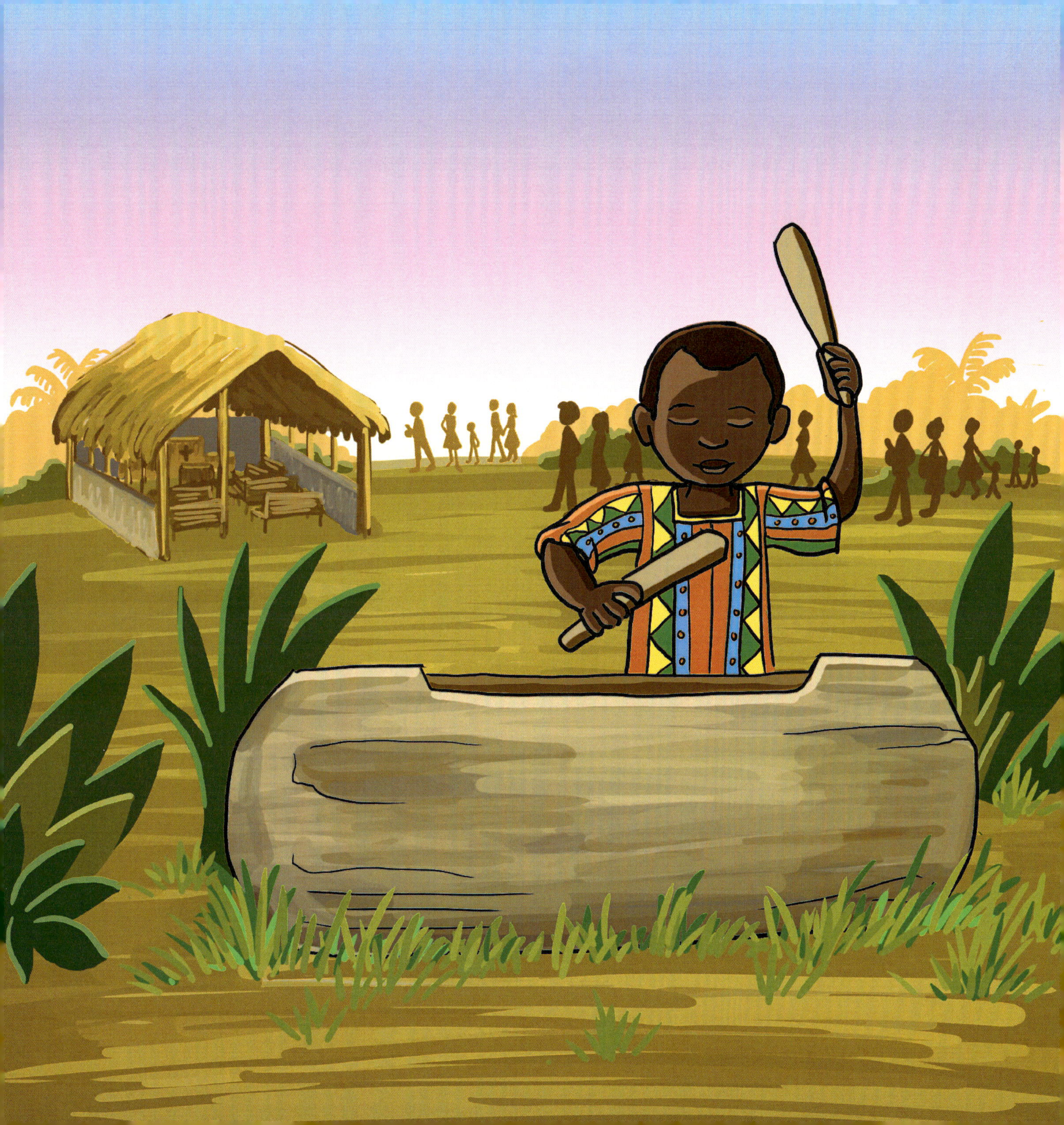

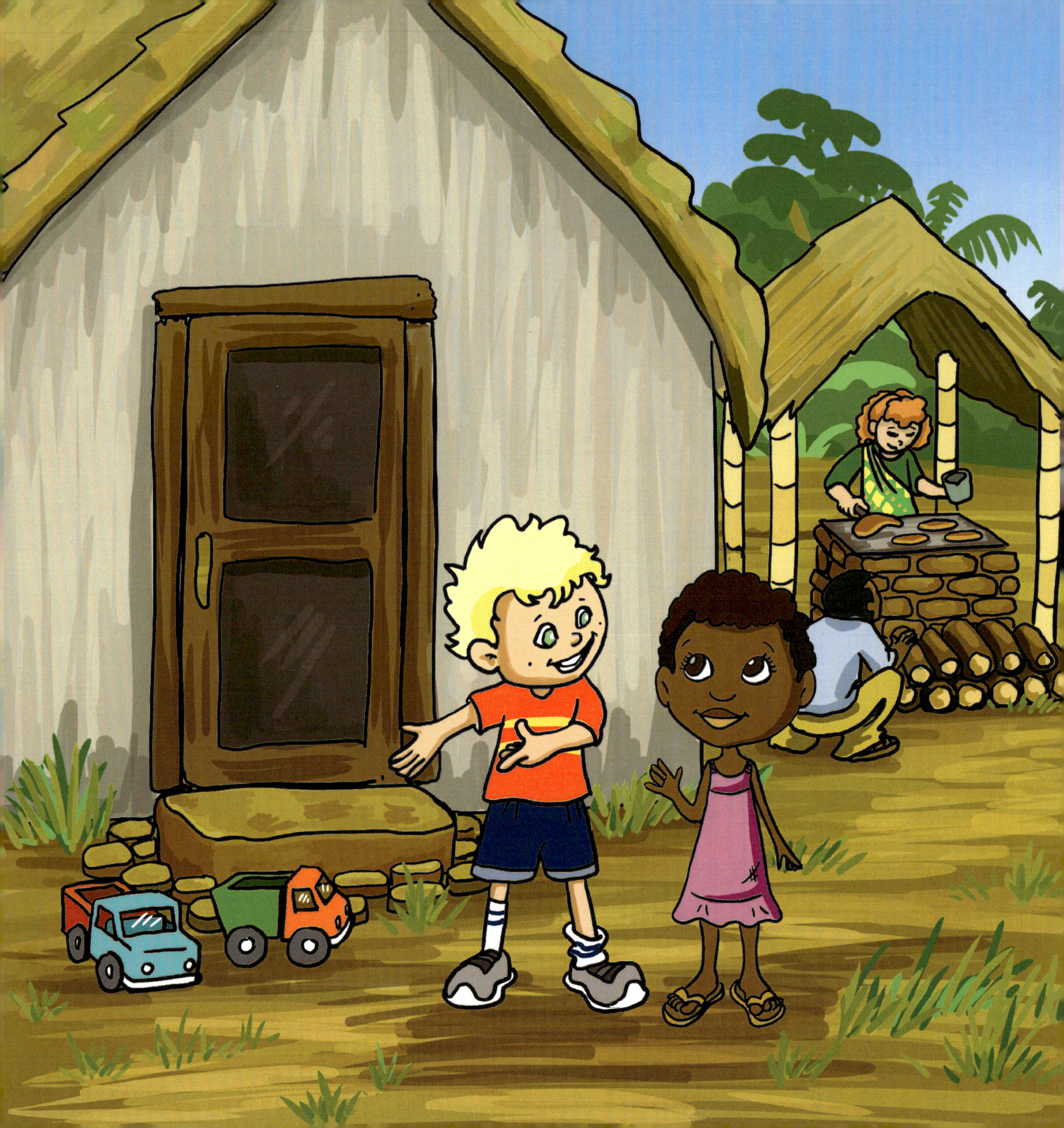

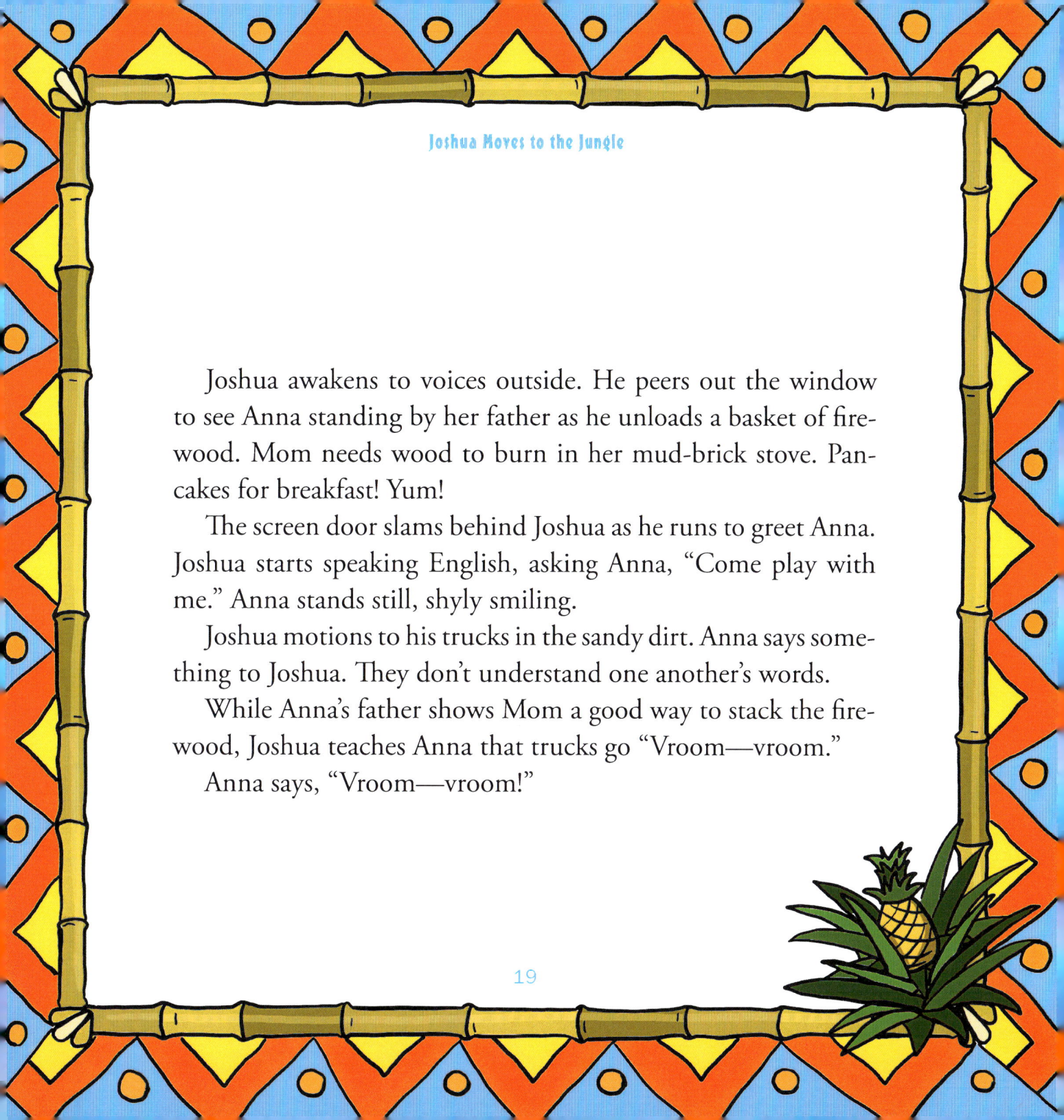

Joshua Moves to the Jungle

Joshua awakens to voices outside. He peers out the window to see Anna standing by her father as he unloads a basket of firewood. Mom needs wood to burn in her mud-brick stove. Pancakes for breakfast! Yum!

The screen door slams behind Joshua as he runs to greet Anna. Joshua starts speaking English, asking Anna, "Come play with me." Anna stands still, shyly smiling.

Joshua motions to his trucks in the sandy dirt. Anna says something to Joshua. They don't understand one another's words.

While Anna's father shows Mom a good way to stack the firewood, Joshua teaches Anna that trucks go "Vroom—vroom."

Anna says, "Vroom—vroom!"

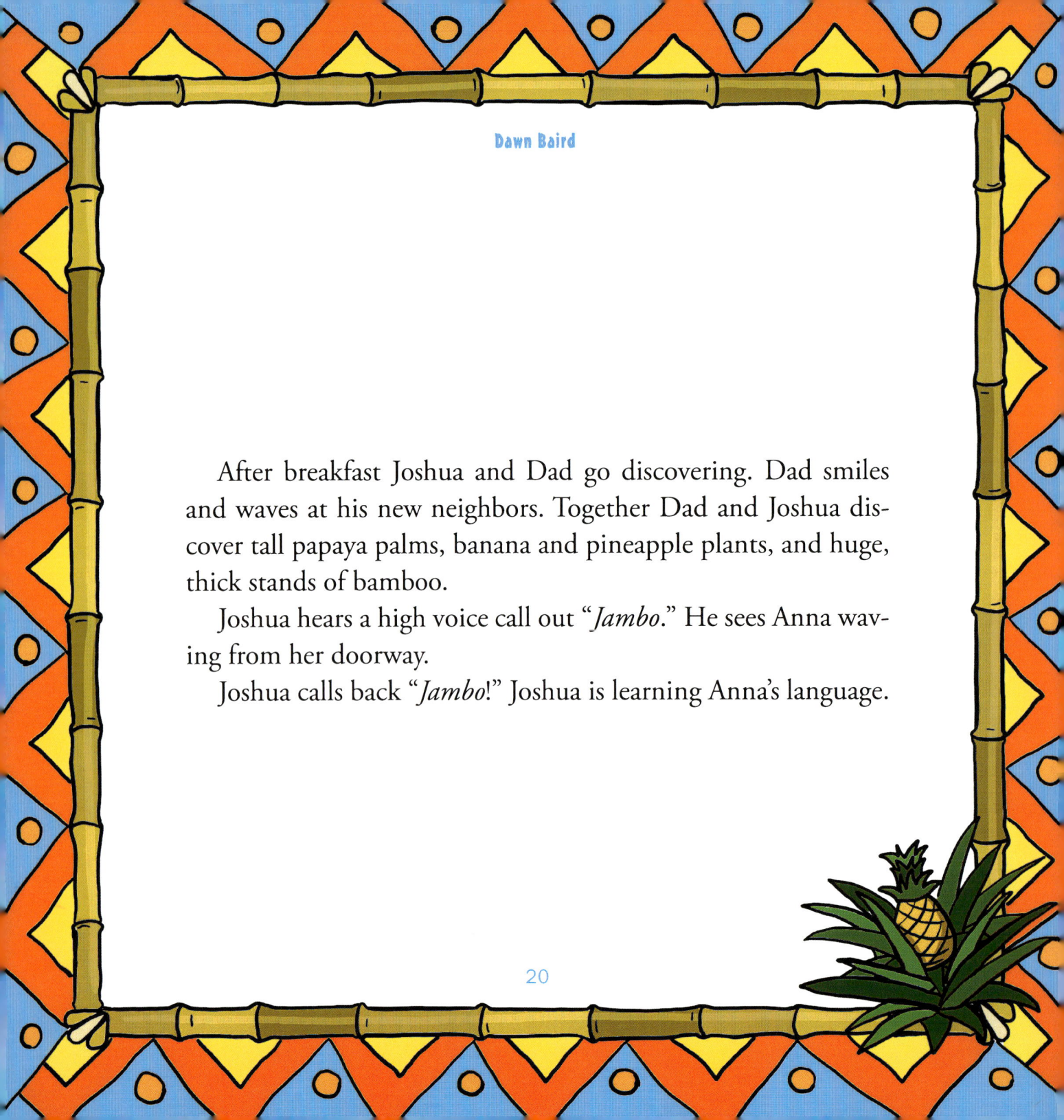

Dawn Baird

After breakfast Joshua and Dad go discovering. Dad smiles and waves at his new neighbors. Together Dad and Joshua discover tall papaya palms, banana and pineapple plants, and huge, thick stands of bamboo.

Joshua hears a high voice call out "*Jambo*." He sees Anna waving from her doorway.

Joshua calls back "*Jambo*!" Joshua is learning Anna's language.

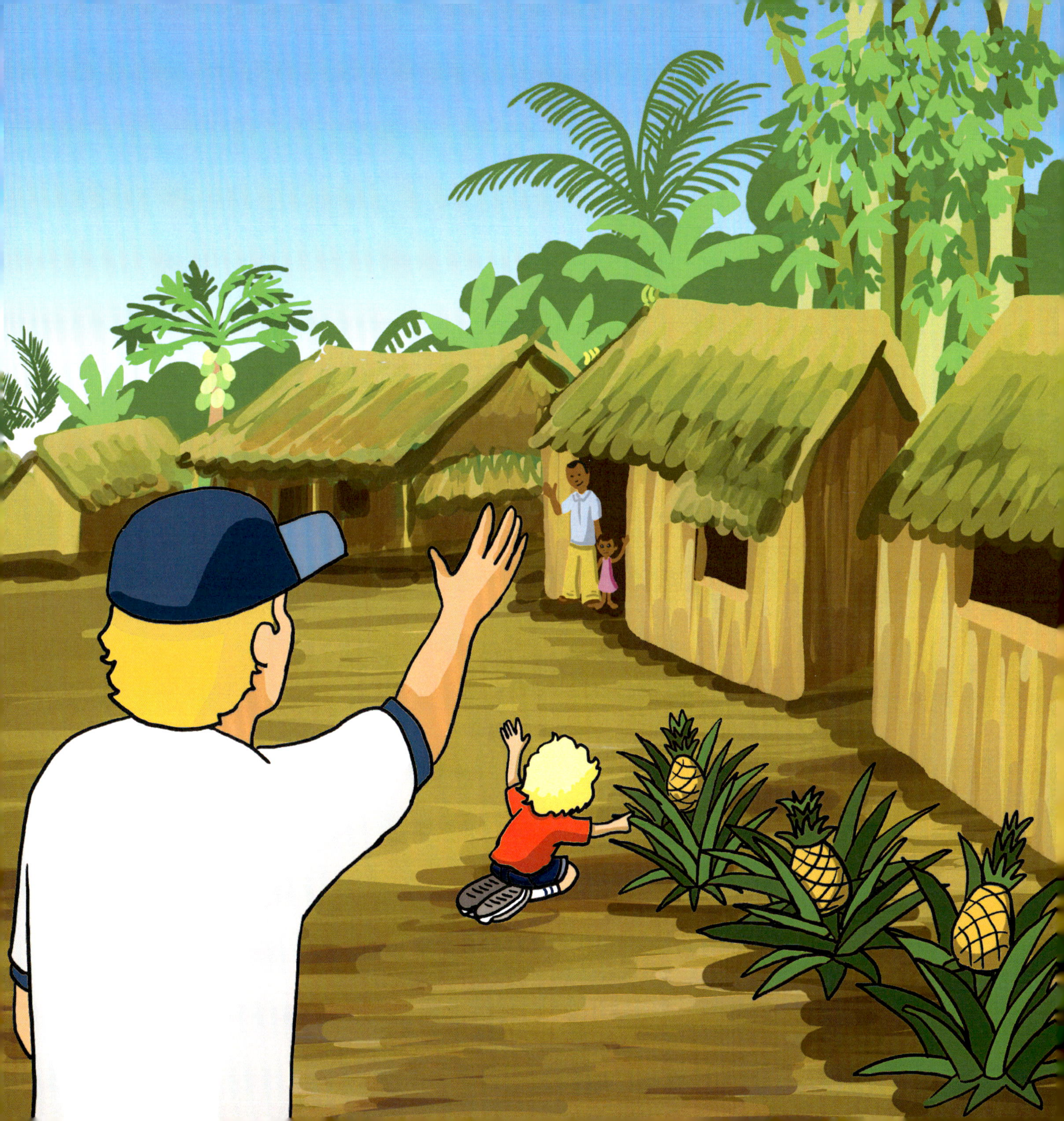

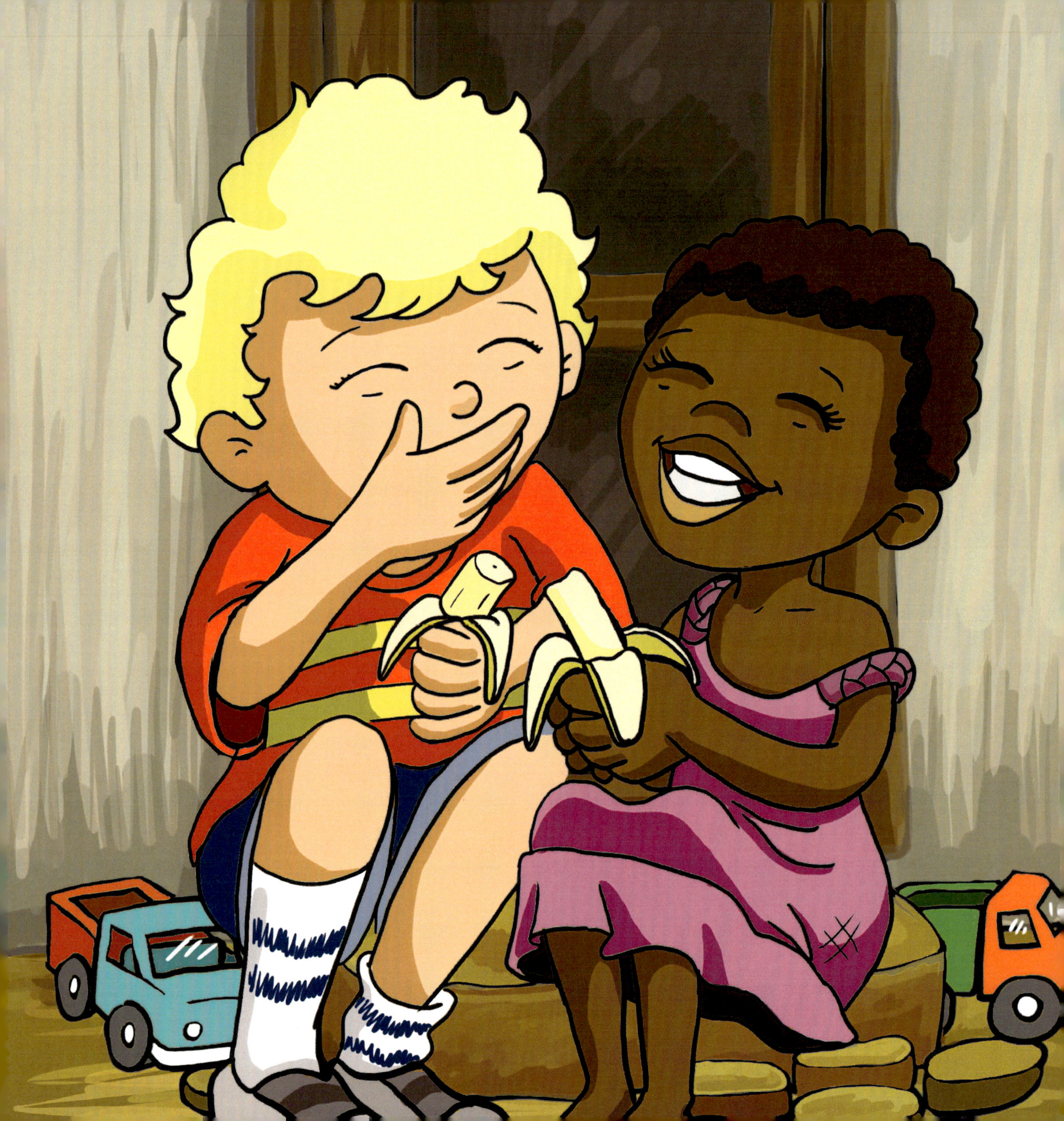

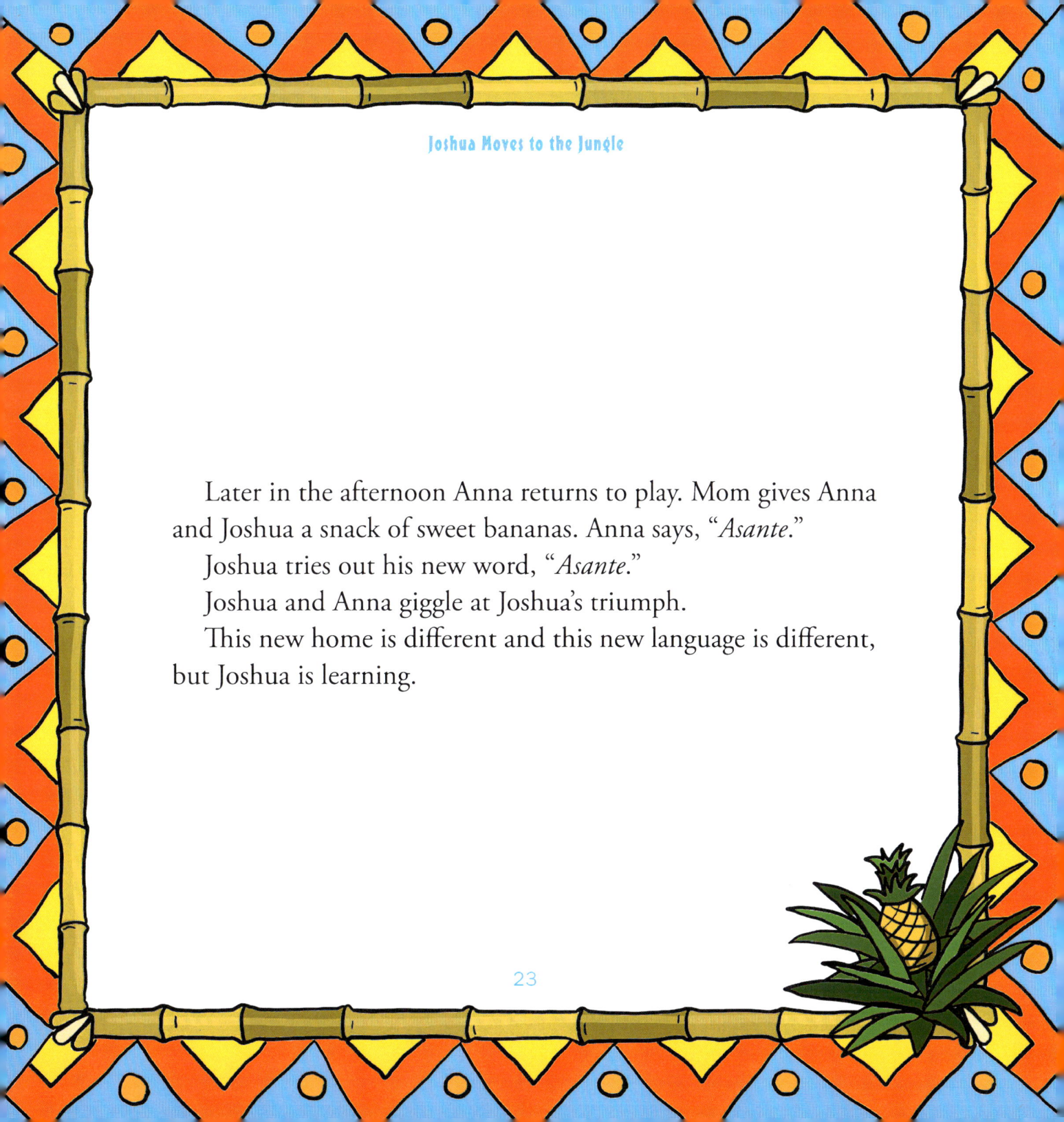

Joshua Moves to the Jungle

Later in the afternoon Anna returns to play. Mom gives Anna and Joshua a snack of sweet bananas. Anna says, "*Asante*."

Joshua tries out his new word, "*Asante*."

Joshua and Anna giggle at Joshua's triumph.

This new home is different and this new language is different, but Joshua is learning.

Dawn Baird

Every day Dad walks the length of the airstrip. Joshua and Anna trot along behind Dad, Mom, Elizabeth, and Rachel.

Dad checks for dangers like holes caused by tarantula nests or footprints left by elephants crossing the airstrip in the night.

The brilliant sun beats hot on Joshua's head. After weeks and months, Joshua still gets hot and sweaty, but he doesn't notice.

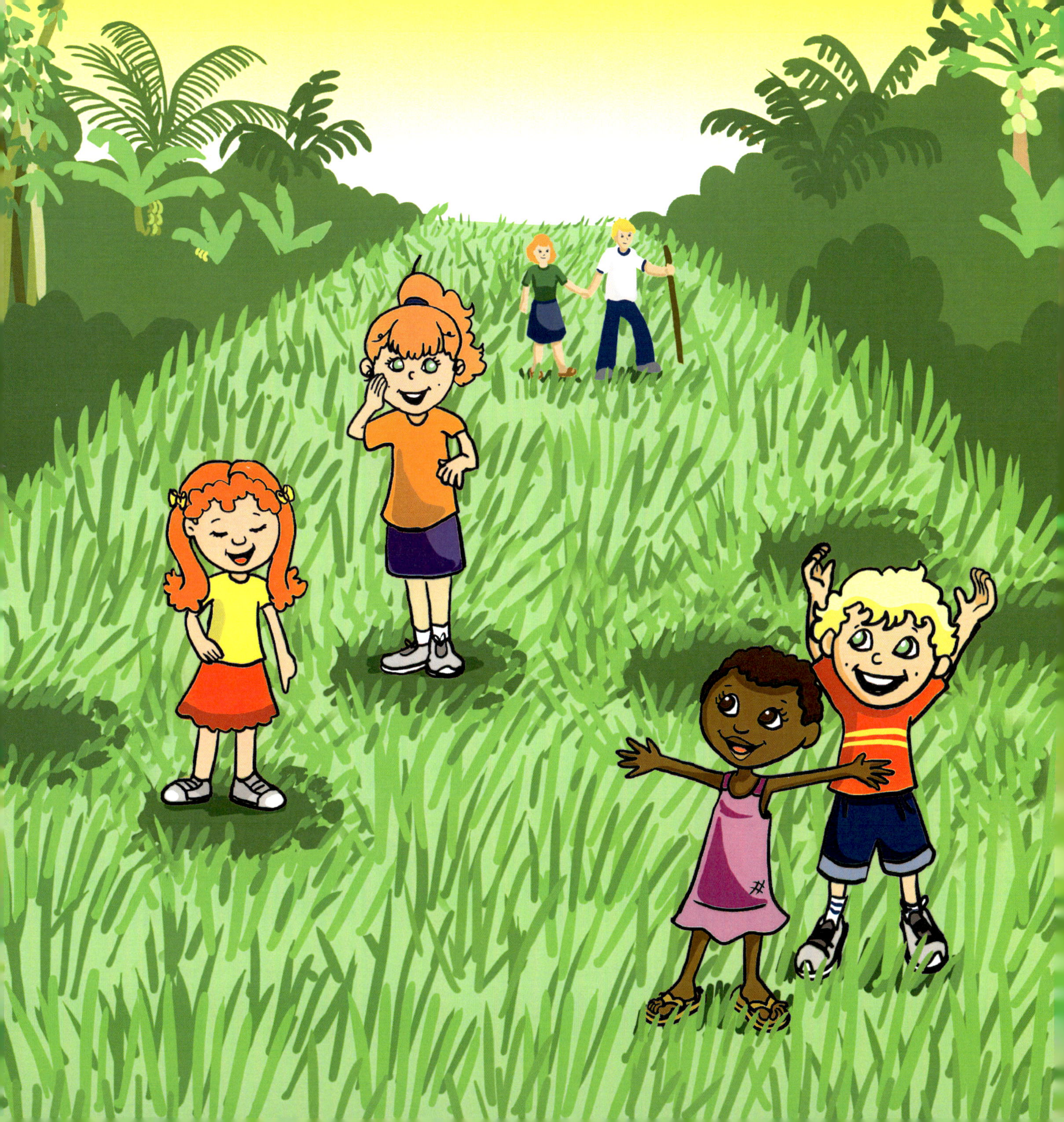

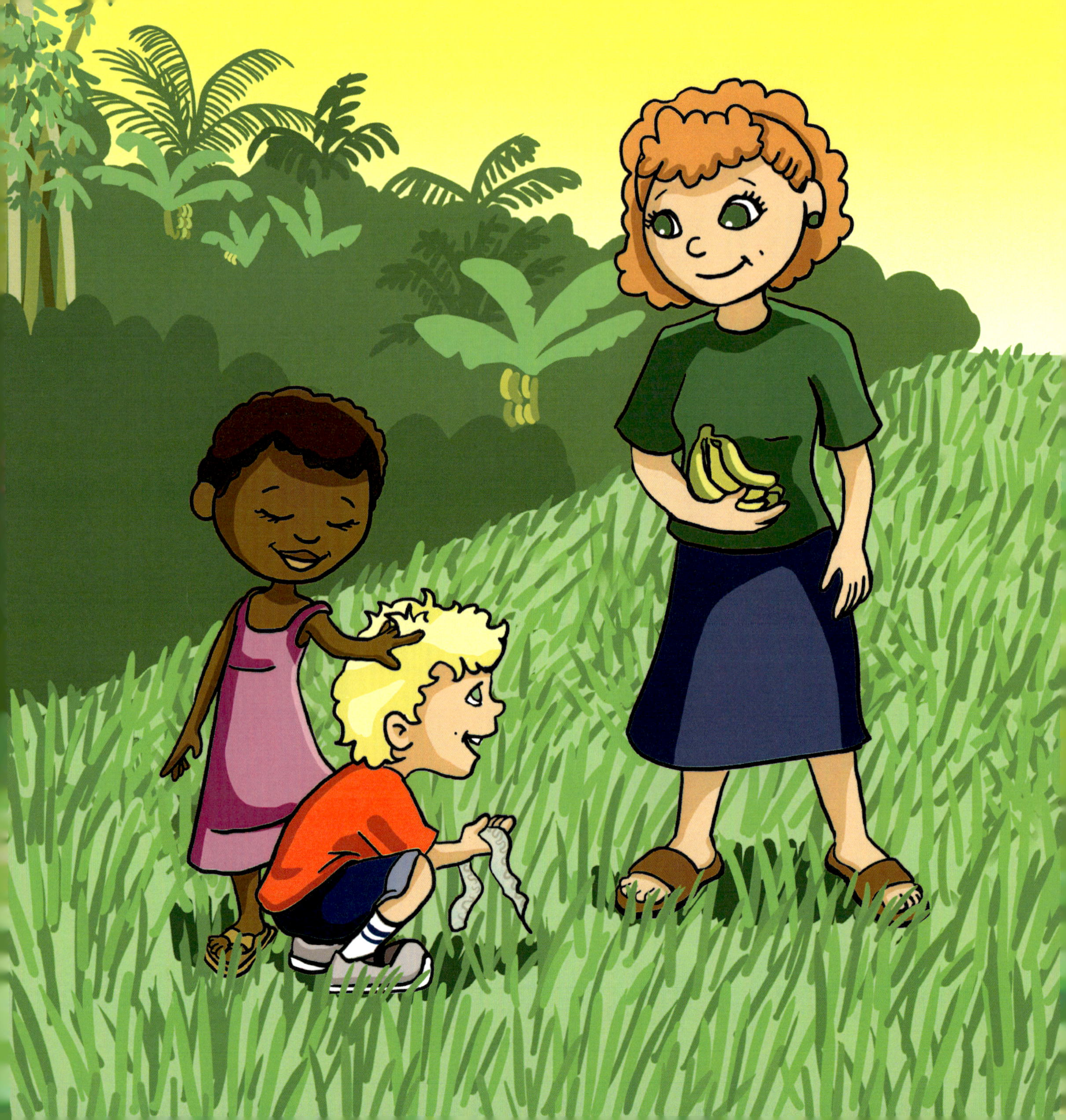

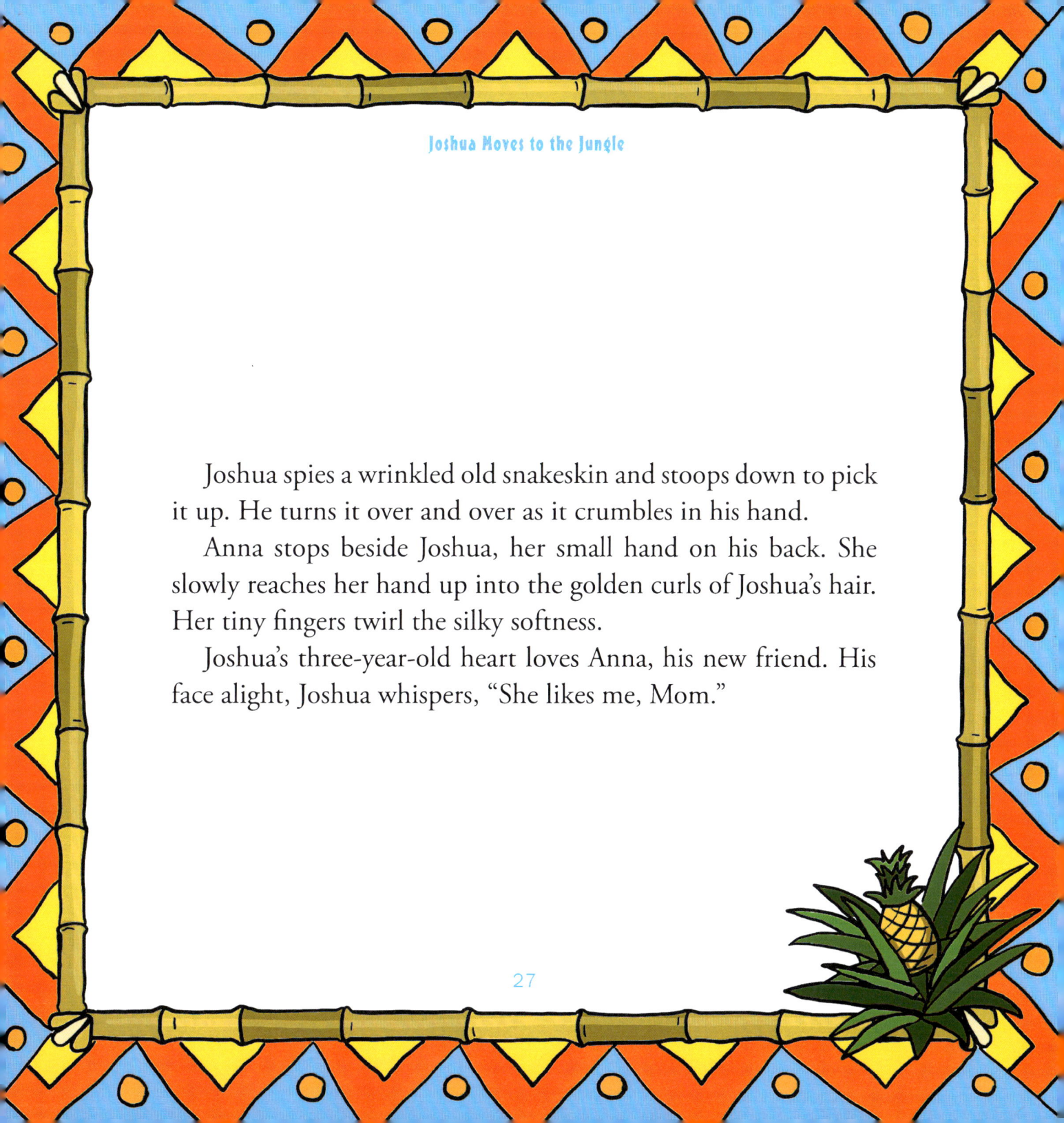

Joshua Moves to the Jungle

Joshua spies a wrinkled old snakeskin and stoops down to pick it up. He turns it over and over as it crumbles in his hand.

Anna stops beside Joshua, her small hand on his back. She slowly reaches her hand up into the golden curls of Joshua's hair. Her tiny fingers twirl the silky softness.

Joshua's three-year-old heart loves Anna, his new friend. His face alight, Joshua whispers, "She likes me, Mom."

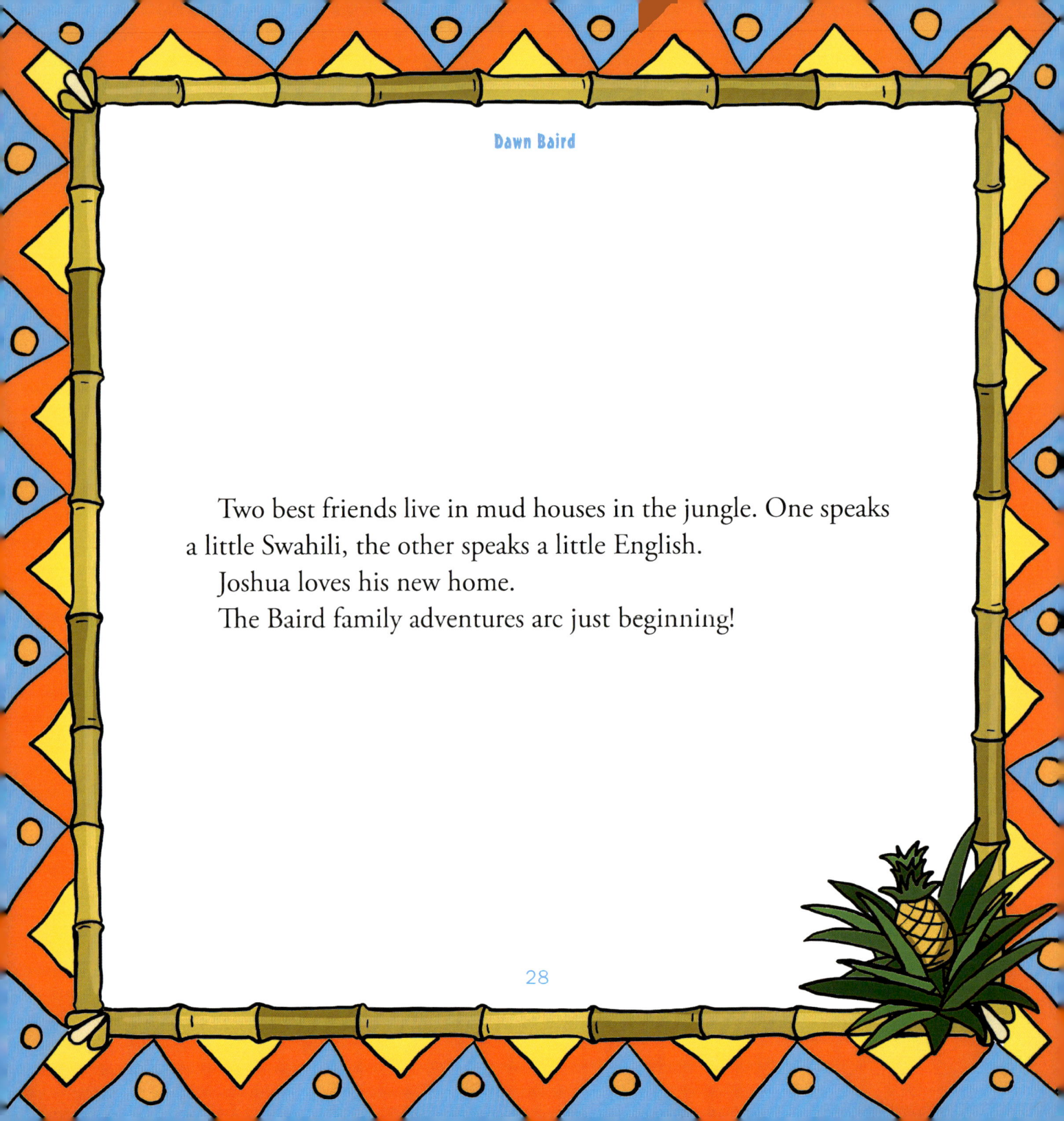

Dawn Baird

Two best friends live in mud houses in the jungle. One speaks a little Swahili, the other speaks a little English.

Joshua loves his new home.

The Baird family adventures arc just beginning!

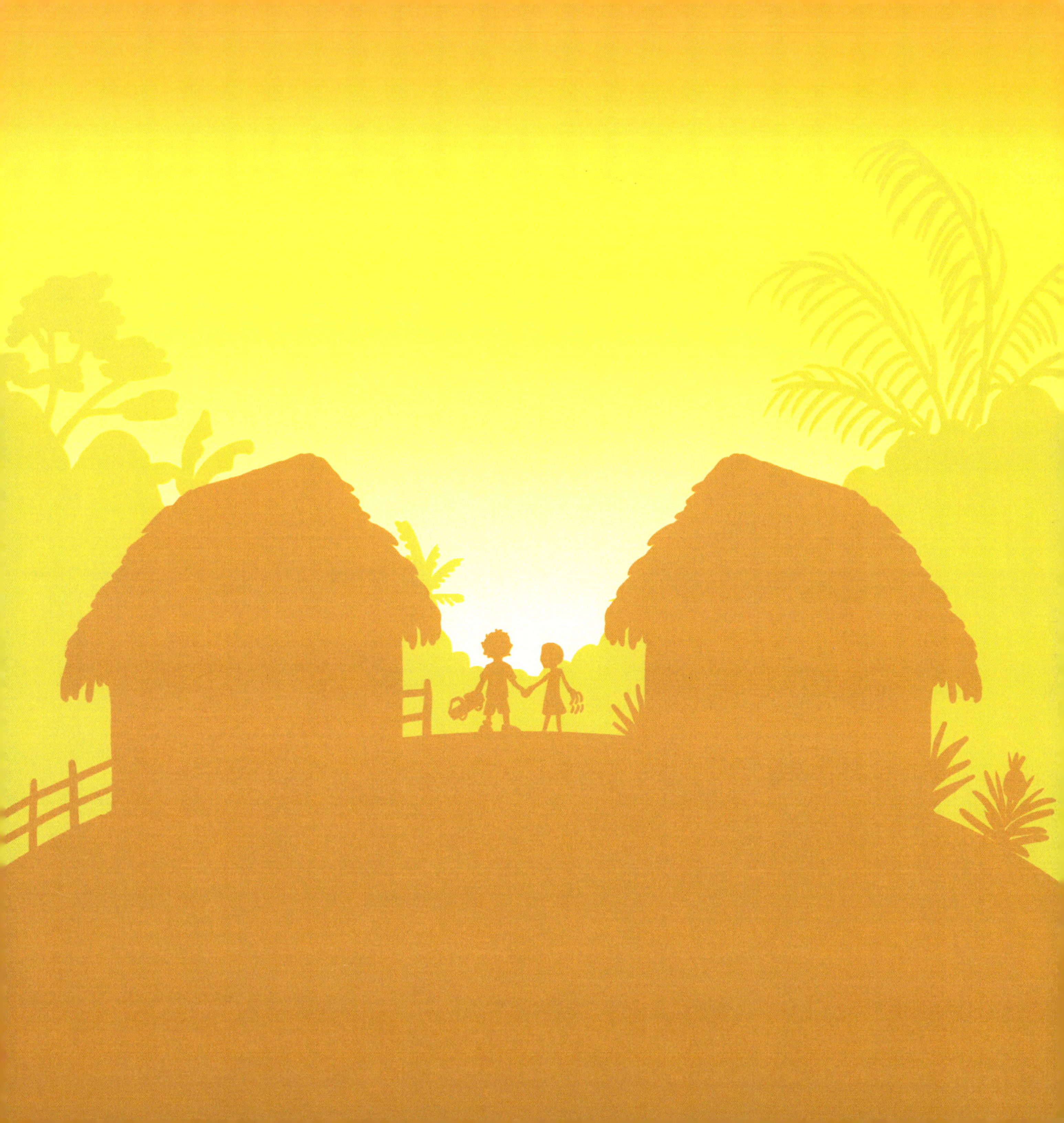

Pronunciation Chart with Definitions

Words are listed as they occur in the story. In all words, place the accent on the next-to-last syllable. The syllables with "ah" like "bah" are to be said like the "ah" in father. The "i" on the end of these words is always a long "e" sound.

Babali   (bah-bah-le)
Definition: an ethnic group in Congo

Bukavu (bu-kah-vu) (long "u" sounds)
Definition: a large city in South Kivu Province on the border of Congo and Rwanda

Bomili (bo-mi-li) (long "o")
Definition: a small village in northern Congo in the Ituri Rain Forest

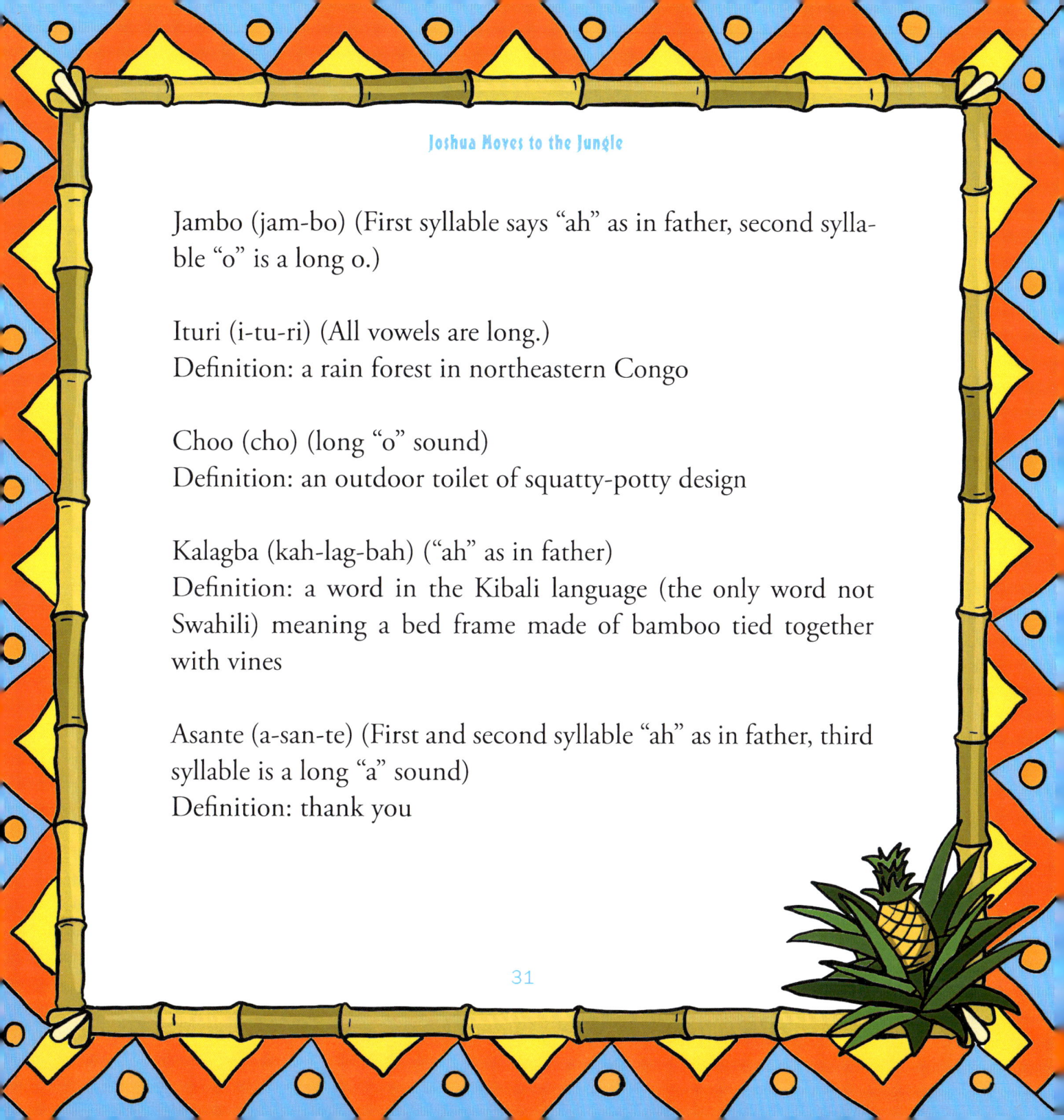

Joshua Moves to the Jungle

Jambo (jam-bo) (First syllable says "ah" as in father, second syllable "o" is a long o.)

Ituri (i-tu-ri) (All vowels are long.)
Definition: a rain forest in northeastern Congo

Choo (cho) (long "o" sound)
Definition: an outdoor toilet of squatty-potty design

Kalagba (kah-lag-bah) ("ah" as in father)
Definition: a word in the Kibali language (the only word not Swahili) meaning a bed frame made of bamboo tied together with vines

Asante (a-san-te) (First and second syllable "ah" as in father, third syllable is a long "a" sound)
Definition: thank you

Bomili – 1982 Dawn and Joshua checking in with coordinator in big city of Bukavu. A regularly scheduled morning contact with the outside world.

Bomili Christian Church – 1983

Bomili 1982 – Old abandoned rubber plantation. Bob, Elizabeth, Rachel and Joshua.

Bomili 1984 – Joshua with Thorin Oakenshield!

Joshua Moves to the Jungle

Bafwasende 1986 – Joshua's 7th birthday, the eggs and pineapple were gifts from Congolese friends. Dawn behind and Rachel holding the pineapple.

Bomili – 1983. A tarantula removed from the Bomili airstrip.

Ituri Rain Forest, early 80's. Climbing to cut down a cluster of palm nuts.

Village of Bafwasende – 1986. Joshua swimming with boys in the creek.

Order Information

REDEMPTION PRESS

To order additional copies of this book, please visit
www.redemption-press.com.
Also available on Amazon.com and BarnesandNoble.com
Or by calling toll free 1-844-2REDEEM.

CPSIA information can be obtained
at www.ICGtesting.com
Printed in the USA
LVXC01n1555231017
553124LV00001B/1